Football and Its Followers

PETE MAY

W

FRANKLIN WATTS
LONDON • SYDNEY

First published in 2004 by Franklin Watts
96 Leonard Street, London EC2A 4XD

Franklin Watts Australia
45-51 Huntley Street
Alexandria, NSW 2015

Copyright © Franklin Watts 2004
Series editor: Rachel Cooke
Series design: White Design
Picture research: Diana Morris

A CIP catalogue record for this book is available from the British Library.

ISBN: 0 7496 5785 5

Printed in Belgium

Acknowledgements:
Action Press/Rex Features: 10, 11.
AP/Topham: 4, 15t. Armando Dadi/Rex Features: 5.
Empics/Topham: 9, 12, 13t, 13b, 15b, 17b, 20, 23, 25, 27.
John Giles/PA/Topham: 8. Robin Hulme/Rex Features: 28.
Chris Lobina/Sporting Pictures (UK) Ltd: front cover.
PA/Topham: 29. Picturepoint/Topham: 7, 22t.
Popperfoto: 6, 18. Pressnet/Topham: 16.
Prosport/Topham: 14, 26. Rex Features: 19, 21.
Sipa/Rex Features: 24. Topham: 17t.
Twentieth Century Fox/Rex Features: 22b.

CONTENTS

THE BEAUTIFUL GAME

FOOTBALL IS THE BIGGEST SPORT in *the world, with a huge influence on society. The Brazilian football star Pelé called it "the beautiful game", and no other sport inspires so many millions of people. It is hard to escape the game's influence: as well as the players and the fans, football can also affect businesses and even governments.*

DO YOU SPEAK FOOTBALL?

Even people who are not football fans often know something about the sport. Teams from England's FA Premiership, Italy's *Serie A* and Spain's *La Liga* are known throughout the world. During the football World Cup – held every four years – huge numbers of people get caught up in the excitement. Football is a universal language, and naming a famous player can help start a conversation anywhere in the world.

Pelé is held aloft by fans after helping Brazil win the 1970 World Cup in Mexico City.

CASHING IN

Football is a massive business. The top clubs, the players, the players' agents and television and newspaper companies can all make huge amounts of cash from the game. Some people think that money and big business are spoiling football. They argue that players' salaries are too high, that fans are exploited and that the top clubs are too wealthy while the rest are too poor. Others point out that the money in football can be used for positive ends, such as building new stadiums and helping local communities.

↑ Italian president Silvio Berlusconi's career in politics has been helped through his ownership of the football club AC Milan.

GET THE FACTS STRAIGHT

A worldwide television audience of 1.1 billion people watched the 2002 World Cup finals held in Japan and South Korea – more than 1 in 6 of the world's population. Top clubs can also attract huge crowds to their stadiums. For example:

- The Spanish club Barcelona's Nou Camp stadium can fit 115,000 fans.
- The Italian San Siro stadium, home of both the AC Milan and Inter Milan clubs, attracts 85,000 supporters for top games.
- The German club Borussia Dortmund has an average of 78,000 spectators for each home match.
- In the 2002–03 season, the English club Manchester United had an average home crowd of 67,630.

BACK TO FRONT

Football used to be reported on the back pages of newspapers, but now the players are front-page news. Stories about England star David Beckham and his pop-star wife Victoria often become a newspaper's lead. Gossip about players' behaviour off the football pitch sells papers and attracts television viewers.

POLITICAL FOOTBALL

Perhaps this is why the worlds of politics and football sometimes merge. Politicians realise that being associated with football can boost their popularity. The British prime minister Tony Blair has been photographed heading a football with the former England manager Kevin Keegan, while Italy's president Silvio Berlusconi named his political party after the football chant *Forza Italia!* ("Come on Italy!").

FOOTBALL IS THE MOST *widely-played – and watched – game in the world. It is played in every continent, and in more than 200 countries. National and international football organisations exist to help develop the sport further. They also organise leagues and tournaments – the most important of which is the World Cup.*

ANYWHERE...

Football's simplicity is a major reason for its popularity. It is open to all and can be played on virtually any surface: even the world's poorest children can play it in the street or on the beach. Its rules are easy, too. Two teams of 11 people play for 90 minutes, with the aim of getting the ball into the other side's goal.

... ANYTIME

Football is often seen as a symbol of normality. In Afghanistan, the football stadium in Kabul was used for public executions by the ruling Taliban. But after the fall of the Taliban in 2002, local residents reclaimed the stadium and played a game against a guest side of foreign footballers. On Christmas Day in 1914, during the First World War, there is evidence that British and German soldiers on the Western Front in Belgium held a truce and played a football match. According to accounts, the Germans won 3–2.

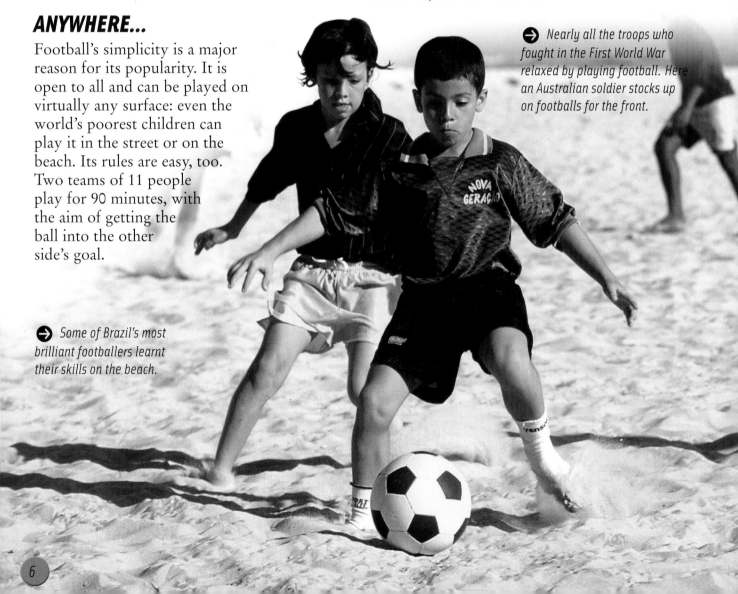

➡ *Nearly all the troops who fought in the First World War relaxed by playing football. Here an Australian soldier stocks up on footballs for the front.*

➡ *Some of Brazil's most brilliant footballers learnt their skills on the beach.*

GOVERNING BODIES

Although it has been played informally for hundreds of years (see box), it was not until the 19th century that the official rules of football were established. Countries set up national leagues, in which groups of clubs competed to win championships. These leagues are governed by national football associations.

THE WORLD CUP

In 1904, the Fédération Internationale de Football Association (FIFA) established itself as football's world governing body. FIFA set up the World Cup in 1930 – by the 1950s the tournament had become a massive success. In 1954, the Union of European Football Associations (UEFA) was formed to govern European competitions. Two years later, UEFA established the European Cup, for which the champions of national leagues in Europe compete.

GET THE FACTS STRAIGHT

The History of Football
- 2500 BC: Chinese records tell of soldiers kicking a ball through bamboo posts in a game called tsu chu.
- 100 BC–AD 400 : Roman soldiers play a game called *harpastum* with a ball, pitch and goals.
- AD 800: Football develops in England as a violent game played between entire villages, using an inflated pig or sheep bladder.
- 1314: King Edward II of England bans football in London for the "many evils" and "great noise" it causes.
- 1530: Citizens of Florence in Italy insist on playing a game of *calcio* – a cross between rugby and football – while under siege by enemies.
- Mid-1800s: Pupils at English public schools such as Eton play organised games of football.
- 1863: English Football Association formed. It adopts the "Cambridge Rules", which establish football and rugby as separate sports.
- 1890s: Organised football spreads through Germany, Holland, Italy, Scandinavia, Hungary, New Zealand, Argentina, Uruguay and many other countries.
- 1930: Hosts Uruguay win the first World Cup.
- 1956: Real Madrid win the first European Cup.
- 2003: 204 countries are members of FIFA.

THE LIFEBLOOD of football is its fans, who support their club passionately whether it is one of the biggest or one of the smallest. Being a fan is a deep emotional commitment, which can result in joy when a team wins a trophy or misery when it suffers heavy defeats or even relegation to a lower league.

➡ *A young fan of West Ham feels the pain when his club is relegated from the English Premier League in the final game of the 2002-03 season.*

LOYAL TO THE END

Once a fan decides to follow a team, he or she usually becomes a lifelong supporter. Some fans feel that clubs exploit this loyalty by charging too much for tickets and replica shirts (see page 10). But fans can be demanding, too. In Italy in 2002, Lazio supporters protested at the club's training ground after the team played badly. In Brazil in 2003, a fan of the Fluminense club released chickens (a symbol of cowardice) on the training ground as a way of criticising the performance of the team.

FOOTBALL RITUALS

Fans show their support for a team in a variety of ways. Supporters buy their club's shirts, hats and scarves to express their loyalty. Pre-match rituals for some fans even involve wearing lucky underpants! Chants, which are sung together at matches, have been part of the fans' identity since the late 1960s. In Italy, Holland and England, fans have even adapted opera arias for use in games. Some supporters also produce their own magazines, known as fanzines, which can attract many readers.

OLD RIVALS

Fans have fierce rivalries with the supporters of other teams. This rivalry is often good-natured, but in its extreme form can also lead to violence (see pages 24-5). Sometimes it is based around religion or history. In Scotland, there have long been tensions between the traditionally Protestant fans of Rangers and the Catholic fans of Celtic. In 1988, when Holland's national football team beat Germany, some Dutch fans threw their bicycles into the air, shouting "We've got our bikes back!" This was a reference to Germany's occupation of Holland in the Second World War, when the Germans confiscated Dutch people's bicycles.

⬇ *Fans of South Korea celebrate their country's unexpected success in the 2002 World Cup.*

FACING THE ISSUES

There is nothing a football fan savours more than triumphing against the odds – and, for non-English fans, beating England at the game it claims to have invented. In 1981, the Norwegian football commentator Bjørge Lillelien famously captured this feeling after Norway beat England in a World Cup qualifying match. In what has been voted the best piece of sporting commentary ever, Lillelien reeled off a list of famous English men and women: "Lord Nelson! Lord Beaverbrook! Winston Churchill! Henry Cooper! Clement Attlee! Anthony Eden! Lady Diana! Maggie Thatcher! Can you hear me Maggie Thatcher? Your boys took one hell of a beating!"

BIG BUSINESS

WITH ITS MILLIONS OF FANS, football has a huge potential for making money. The European football market is worth an estimated £10 billion. Some top clubs have become public limited companies, and the fate of a manager or a player can depend on share prices as much as results. However, football is not necessarily an efficient business: even if a club spends a fortune on its players, there is no guarantee it will win matches.

WHAT DO YOU THINK?

Replica football shirts are big earners. They are cheap to make, but can be sold in clubs' souvenir shops for a lot of money. Some clubs that sign expensive, world-famous players can nearly make their money back just by selling these new players' replica shirts. Since the 1990s, people have accused big clubs of changing their kit every season so that fans will keep buying new shirts.

- Do you think clubs need to change their kit designs every season?
- Think of some reasons that clubs may use to defend the price of their replica shirts. Do you think any of these are fair?

MERCHANDISING

Large clubs gain most of their income from selling the rights to televise matches (see pages 12-3). But another source of income is merchandising. Since the 1990s, many top clubs have opened huge stores, selling everything from replica shirts to mouse-mats. Manchester United's income from merchandising is more than the entire revenue of the English third division. The club even has stores in Japan and China.

← *When David Beckham signed for Real Madrid, Spanish flans flocked to buy replica shirts with his name on. The Spanish club signed Beckham partly because of the merchandising income he would generate.*

SPONSORSHIP

A third major source of income is sponsorship. The big clubs' sponsors are usually multinational companies, wishing to benefit from being linked with a successful team. In Germany, Bayern Munich's sponsorship deal with T-mobile is worth £11 million a year, while Spain's Real Madrid makes £8 million a year from Siemens. Some clubs have a long history with one sponsor. In Holland, PSV Eindhoven began as an amateur club for employees of the electronics company Philips. Today, PSV (which stands for Philips Sport Vereniging) play at the Philips Stadium.

⬇ *Players for Dutch club PSV Eindhoven sport the Philips name on their shirts.*

LIFE AFTER DEBT

Many clubs spend most of their income on players' wages. Some people think these wages are too high and can lead to big problems. In 2001, the English club Leeds United reached the semi-final of the European Champions League. Two years later, however, Leeds, having spent too much on players, were in debt by around £100 million. Unwise spending had even worse consequences for the Italian side Fiorentina. In 2002, this former Serie A club was thrown out of the Italian football league because its debts were so great. In 2004, another Italian side, Parma, faced bankruptcy after the collapse of owner Calisto Tanzi's business empire.

FOOTBALL AND TELEVISION

TELEVISION HAS BECOME *the single most important factor in football. With the emergence of satellite and cable television in the early 1990s, the value of the rights for televised football matches soared. Once, only big international matches and cup finals were shown on live television, but now there are channels with 24-hour coverage of the sport, and some clubs even have their own channels.*

⊕ *TV cameras can now be seen at every top football match.*

TELLY RULES

Some people think that television has too big an influence on football. In 2002, Italian fans were angry when the start of the country's football season was delayed because of a breakdown in the top clubs' negotiations with TV companies for more money. A more positive aspect of TV coverage is that players are no longer able to get away with violence in games: video evidence can reveal bad behaviour, even when the referee has missed the incident.

A EUROPEAN SUPERLEAGUE?

Successful clubs can earn huge sums of money from TV rights. For instance, a place in the European Champions League can generate up to £20 million extra income. More and more European clubs want to join this league, but some people fear that the end result will be a "superleague", with clubs that are not members having less money to attract top players or win new supporters.

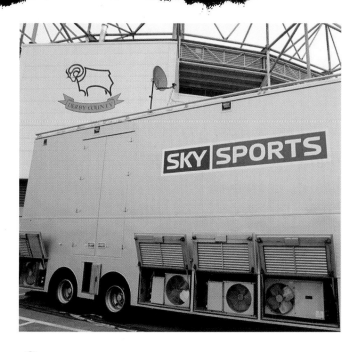

↑ *TV companies such as Sky Sports base their appeal on live football coverage and have brought huge sums of money into the game.*

MONEY PROBLEMS

The importance of TV revenue means that if a team is relegated – for example, if it goes down from the first to the second division – it faces a potentially disastrous loss of income. A related problem is that clubs can rely too heavily on TV income. In 2002, the collapse of the Kirch TV empire in Germany and the ITV Digital company in Britain left a number of clubs facing possible bankruptcy.

SWITCH ON, SWITCH OFF

Fans love to watch live games on television, often in bars. But many of them believe that TV companies are too powerful. They feel that they are not consulted when the companies change match days and kick-off times to gain the best pay-per-view TV audience. They also think that television results in low crowd numbers at matches, because people watch games at home instead. Yet TV coverage also means that casual supporters and those who are not fit enough to attend games do not miss the action.

WHAT DO YOU THINK?

- Do you think people should pay money to see sporting events on television? Think of two reasons why they should and two reasons why they should not.
- Why do you think television companies are prepared to pay so much to show matches?
- Why do some people think that football matches should only be shown on television after they have taken place, and not live?

→ *Juventus manager Marcello Lippi (right) is interviewed after a match. These interviews are usually agreed as part of a club's deal with the TV companies.*

CLUBS HAVE TWO MAIN WAYS to get hold of new footballers – signings and transfers. Signings are made with players who do not have a contract with another club. A transfer, on the other hand, is when one club sells a player to another club. These sales can involve enormous sums.

DOUBLE AGENTS

Transfers and new signings are tempting for managers because they can provide a quick fix if a team is performing badly. The arrival of a famous player at a club is also exciting for the fans, and can show that the club is ambitious for success. But a lot of fans think there is too much buying and selling of players. Players' agents take a percentage of any transfer fee, and some people accuse agents of encouraging their players to move purely for financial gain.

LOCAL TALENT?

Some clubs sign so many players from abroad that they have none from their local area, or even their own country. In 1999, Chelsea made history by fielding the first ever all-foreign side in England. It contained two players each from Italy and France, a Dutchman, a Romanian, a Spaniard, a Brazilian, a Uruguayan, a Nigerian and a Norwegian. Some fans argue that this practice discourages local young people from becoming footballers, but others regard it as another aspect of the modern global economy.

← In 2001, French superstar Zinedine Zidane transferred to Real Madrid from Juventus for a record fee of £46.5 million.

→ Chelsea made football history by fielding a team with no British players against Southampton in 1999.

YOUNG AT HEART

The alternative to buying a team is to develop young players through youth sides. Footballers who have been at a club since they were junior players may be more loyal and try harder than expensive signings with no loyalty to a local team. Another advantage of developing young players is that they cost nothing. A good youth policy can save a club millions of pounds and, if those young players are later sold, the club makes a healthy profit. Many small clubs survive by developing and selling young talent.

➡ *Celtic win the 1967 European Cup. All 11 players in the victorious team were born in or around Glasgow.*

FACING THE ISSUES

Buying players – or a whole club – is a way to raise the buyers' profiles. In the summer of 2003 the Russian oil millionaire Roman Abramovich, one of the richest men in the world, bought the heavily indebted English club Chelsea FC. In less than two months he bought nine world class players for a total of around £100 million. This spree generated huge headlines. Before his move into football few people outside Russia had heard of Abramovich; now the whole of Europe knew who he was.

MIXING IT UP

Success cannot always be bought. Teams have to be built up over several years, and the mix of new players and local talent has to generate the right team spirit. Top sides like Barcelona and Manchester United have always tried to keep a core of home-grown players who grew up together, alongside the more expensive foreign players.

FOOTBALLERS INCLUDE AMATEUR and part-time players, relatively low-paid professionals to millionaire superstars. These stars are treated as fashion icons by the media and are adored by their young fans, but they can have problems dealing with their wealth and fame.

IT'S TOUGH AT THE TOP

For top footballers the rewards are great. Clubs try to attract the best players by offering the highest wages, and superstars can earn as much as £80,000 a week. These players can earn even more money when their images are used in advertising. In 2003, David Beckham earned approximately £10 million – double his reported £5 million salary at Real Madrid – from helping to advertise products such as football boots and trainers, mobile phones and sunglasses.

WHAT DO YOU THINK?

Top players often earn more in a week than most people do in a year.

- Do footballers' short careers justify them being paid so much more?
- Would players be more motivated if they had to play from a love of the game rather than a love of cash?
- Until 1961, English footballers' earnings were restricted by a maximum wage regulation. Do you think there is a case for bringing this back?

⬆ English superstar David Beckham, pictured with his pop-star wife Victoria, gets almost as much press coverage for his clothes as he does for his football.

THE NEW POP STARS

Today, many people associate footballers with lavish lifestyles. Newspapers and magazines often show pictures of players with glamorous girlfriends, and discuss their clothes, homes and cars. Even the players seem to expect other footballers to adopt a materialistic lifestyle. For example, when the German striker Jurgen Klinsmann drove a small, inexpensive car, he was ridiculed by his team-mates.

PAYING A PRICE

Many players do not cope well with wealth and celebrity. The brilliant Argentinean footballer Diego Maradona came from a poor part of Buenos Aires and became possibly the best player in the world in the 1980s. However, he turned to alcohol and cocaine as an escape from the pressure of his position. In the 1990s he twice failed drugs tests, including during the 1994 World Cup finals, when he was sent home in disgrace.

 Lower league clubs face a circular problem: poor crowds mean they cannot pay better players to attract more fans.

➡ Maradona celebrates wildly after his team scores against Greece in the 1994 World Cup. He failed a drugs test after the match.

SHORT CAREERS

Players and their agents argue that they deserve large salaries because football is a short career – few play professionally beyond the age of 35. They also argue that footballers can lose their livelihood through just one injury, and that stars in other sports also earn huge sums.

FEET ON THE GROUND

But not all footballers are rich. As more money goes to the top clubs, players in the lower leagues have suffered. Their earnings are much closer to – or lower than – fans' wages. Unless a wealthy owner brings money to a small club, this situation is very hard to change. However, some commentators argue that this gives lower league matches a genuine quality lacking in higher divisions – the players are participating for love of the game rather than a large wage packet.

YOUNG FANS REGARD *their football heroes as role models, so it is important that these players set a good example. But footballers do not always behave well. They are often passionate, competitive people, who in the heat of a match can misbehave. Off the pitch they can also act badly, but unlike ordinary people the media will publicise any mistakes they make.*

SPITTING IMAGE

If players act too aggressively during matches the referee can send them off by showing them a red card. For lesser offences, the referee will show a player a yellow card, but if a player gets two yellow cards he must also leave the pitch. One of the most notorious moments in World Cup history was in 1990, when Holland's Frank Rijkaard spat at Germany's Rudi Voller after the German player fouled him. Both players were sent off (pictured left).

KICK THE BALL, NOT THE FAN

One of the most irresponsible things a footballer can do is fight with supporters. In 1995, the Manchester United player Eric Cantona attacked a Crystal Palace fan who had shouted obscenities at him. Cantona's behaviour could have started a riot, and the pictures of his assault made front-page news. He was suspended for eight months and sentenced to 120 hours community service. To his credit, Cantona came back to help Manchester United win the English cup and championship.

← *Germany's Rudi Voller and Holland's Frank Rijkaard are sent off in a 1990 World Cup match.*

↑ *Having already been shown the red card, Eric Cantona aims a kick at Crystal Palace fan Matthew Simmons.*

ALCOHOL AND WORSE

Footballers are also liable to temptation off the pitch. Successful young players can earn huge wages, but often do not receive enough advice on how to handle wealth and adulation (see page 17). In Germany, Holland and Britain there has been a tradition of team bonding through alcohol, and footballers have been involved in scandals including nightclub fights, drug-taking, drink-driving, match-fixing and rape allegations. Footballers in countries such as Italy and Spain have less problems with drinking, and have provided other players with an example of a more professional attitude. Despite the headlines and the scandals, the majority of players do behave well.

FACING THE ISSUES

The press have an ambivalent relationship with soccer stars. They complain about their bad behaviour but then use stories about it to sell their papers. A good example of the resulting double standards was the media furore that followed an accusation of rape against two Premiership footballers after an incident in a hotel room in London in September 2003. For days the tabloid papers and internet sites contained lurid accounts of what went on and speculation about the identities of the players involved. Some people feel the press is as responsible for football's "bad boy" image as the players themselves.

FOOTBALL CLUBS *have a huge effect on their local communities. For example, a successful team can help draw industry and investment to an area that might otherwise be ignored. Many small firms depend on a football club for their existence, while bigger companies often find that a major win by a local team motivates their employees.*

LOCAL ROOTS

Clubs can be a focus for local pride. For many years Real Sociedad, a club in the Basque region of northern Spain, recruited only Basque-born players. This policy created a strong bond with the club's fans, in a region that wished to emphasise its separateness from Spain. Another way of linking football to the community is when a stadium is owned by the local council. The people of Milan in Italy regard the San Siro Stadium – home of both Inter and AC Milan – as a community asset.

GIVING BACK

A club depends on its supporters for survival. When the Spanish side Deportivo Alavés qualified for the UEFA Cup for the first time, the club said "thank you" to its fans by printing a commemorative shirt that included the names of all 13,400 season ticket holders. Another club giving something back to the community is Steaua Bucharest of Romania. In 2003, the club's owner, Giga Becali, promised to build a new church for every UEFA Cup match his side won.

⬇ *Real Sociedad players. Although no longer exclusively Basque, the team still favours local talent.*

↑ *Flowers and scarves laid out at the Anfield Stadium in memory of the Liverpool fans who died at Hillsborough. The tragedy emphasised the bond between the club and the local community.*

CROSSING BOUNDARIES

Many football clubs try to support their local communities in other ways. They send players and coaches out to help children with learning difficulties or physical disabilities play football. Disadvantaged young people are often invited not only to train at clubs, but also to use computers and do homework there. In England, clubs like West Ham and Leicester have policies of attempting to reach out to the local Asian communities, encouraging them to play and watch football. Even in countries scared by war, such as Sierra Leone, clubs help children disabled by landmines to play the game.

FACING THE ISSUES

Tragedy can bring a community and a club even closer together. In 1989, 96 Liverpool fans died at the Hillsborough Stadium in Sheffield during an FA Cup semi-final. The deaths were caused by severe overcrowding in the standing area set aside for Liverpool fans. Part of the problem was that the police on duty miscalculated the number of fans who could fit into this area, and regarded the people trying to escape onto the pitch as hooligans rather than fans fighting for their lives. Following the disaster, members of the public laid thousands of wreaths outside the gates of Liverpool's own Anfield Stadium, and the club's players and manager attended the funerals of the victims.

FOOTBALL IS *often regarded as a male sport, but it has always been played by women. Some of the first games of village football in medieval Europe were between married and unmarried women. Today, there are more than 30 million registered female players worldwide. In the United States, where football is seen as a unisex game, nearly half of all players are women.*

➔ *An artist depicts Dick Kerr's Ladies playing a floodlit match in the 1920s.*

TACKLING PREJUDICE

Like the male game, organised women's football became popular in the late 19th century. During and after the First World War, a women's team from Preston in England, called Dick Kerr's Ladies, attracted huge crowds for matches, including 53,000 for a game in 1920. But in 1921 the English Football Association ruled that the sport was "unsuited for females", and banned women's football from professional clubs' grounds. Germany and Holland both banned women's football in 1955. By the 1970s, however, the women's game had made a comeback, and these outdated bans were removed. Today, women's football is growing in popularity.

◀ *The hit film **Bend It Like Beckham** explored some of the difficulties – and joys – encountered by women playing football today.*

A GROWING SPORT

The first women's World Cup was held in China in 1991. The final, which the USA won, was watched by 65,000 fans. In Germany there are more than half a million registered women players, while in England there are around 85,000. Women's football has received some coverage on television, but still has far fewer supporters than the men's game. Until large numbers of fans attend their matches, female teams will not attract the same sponsorship or television deals as their male counterparts.

WOMEN IN MEN'S FOOTBALL

The men's game has benefited from women's growing interest in football – there are many more female fans for example. Women have also gained positions of influence at clubs. Karren Brady, for instance, is the managing director of Birmingham City. A growing number of football commentators in the media are women.

➡ *Italian international Patrizia Panico. In Italy many women's sides are semi-professional.*

WHAT DO YOU THINK?

● In 2004, Sepp Blatter, president of FIFA, said: "Let the women play in more feminine clothes like they do in volleyball. They could for example have tighter shorts." He felt this would attract fans to women's football. What do you think?

● Women's sides will never be as big or as physically strong as all-male teams, but their games are just as competitive. Should men and women play in the same sides or compete in separate leagues?

● Do you think a woman will ever play for one of the world's most famous male clubs?

HOOLIGANS

THERE HAS ALWAYS been some violence associated with football, right back to the medieval games when property would be smashed and many people injured. However, the 1970s saw the rise across Europe of a new type of football violence, known as hooliganism. This violence was extremely damaging to the sport's reputation.

WHAT ARE THEY PLAYING AT?

Supporting a football team is like being part of a tribe. Football hooligans take this tribal aspect to an extreme. During home matches they take pride in defending their territory against opposition fans; at away matches they may "invade" or "take" the opposition's territory by standing in their part of the stadium. Hooliganism can range from shouting abuse and hurling objects to large-scale fighting and rioting. Some hooligans do it to impress their peers. Successful fighting against opposition fans means that hooligans gain respect from their mates.

← *Juventus fans in violent clashes before the Heysel Stadium disaster of 1985.*

⬇ *Fanatical Lazio fans set off flares in the crowd. Such provocative actions can lead to violence.*

In his autobiography, the Italian footballer Paolo Di Canio described his teenage years as an Ultra supporter of Lazio:
"When you're in a group, a mob, you feel invincible. Any type of fear or apprehension you may have had dissolves as you feel the power of the mob flowing through you. It didn't matter, we were never scared, no matter how dangerous things became. I've had rocks and bricks hurled at me by rival fans. I've been teargassed and clubbed by the police, I've seen things I wish I hadn't. I have lived the life of the travelling Ultra and, all told, I'm glad I did."
From: Paolo Di Canio: The Autobiography (HarperCollins, 2000)

TRAGEDY STRIKES

Hooliganism can have terrible consequences. A devastating outbreak of violence during the 1985 European Cup final resulted in disaster at the Heysel Stadium in Belgium. When Liverpool fans charged at supporters of the Italian team Juventus, a wall collapsed and 39 innocent Italians were killed.

PREVENTING VIOLENCE

The problem of hooliganism has eased since the 1980s for a number of reasons. These include: all-seater stadiums, which restrict the chances for fighting; closed circuit TV cameras inside stadiums, which film suspected troublemakers; better policing; and an increase in the number of women attending matches. But the problem has not entirely gone away. Since the 1990s, hooliganism has increased in former communist countries in Europe, such as Poland and Hungary.

GANGING UP

Groups of fighting fans have their own informal leaders and military-style nicknames. In England, names of football gangs have included the Chelsea Headhunters, the West Ham Inter-City Firm and the Millwall F Troop. In Italy, hooligans are known as Ultras. Organised hooligan supporters of Italy's Lazio team are called the *Irriducibili* (meaning "unyielding").

PATRIOTISM OR RACISM?

HOLLAND FANS forming a wall of orange shirts; Danish supporters clad in imitation Viking helmets: this is all part of the spectacle of international football. Many fans express patriotic feelings at matches against teams from other nations. But there are sometimes moments when fans move beyond patriotism to xenophobia and racism – the hatred of people from different countries and cultures.

➡ *Dutch fans express their patriotism by painting their faces, singing and playing drums. Everyone enjoys the carnival atmosphere.*

WHAT DO YOU THINK?

- Should countries with racist followers be banned from international tournaments? What problems could result from this ban?
- Would we be better off without international football matches altogether?
- Can fighting over football ever be justified?
- How would you punish people who expressed racism at football matches?

SHAMEFUL BEHAVIOUR

In the 1980s and 1990s, England international games frequently attracted hooligans. Some of these people belonged to racist organisations such as the British National Party or the National Front. During matches, racists have made Nazi salutes, sung racist chants and booed black players. This kind of behaviour and rioting led to English fans being banned from some stadiums and heavy (some say excessive) policing of fans. But racism is not exclusive to England. In 2003, UEFA conducted an inquiry into the racist abuse of England's black players during a match in Macedonia. Players, too, can be racist. Lazio's Sinisa Mihajlovic publicly apologised for his racist abuse of Arsenal's black midfielder Patrick Vieira in a Champions League game in 2000.

AN INTERNATIONAL PROBLEM

Football violence may be labelled "the English disease", but there is always a risk of violent behaviour at matches between teams from different countries. In 1992, when Holland played Germany, in the Dutch border town of Enschede, rival fans hurled glasses and rocks at each other. In 2000, Turkish fans of the Galatasaray team stabbed to death two Leeds United supporters before a UEFA Cup match. Football can even start wars. In 1969, El Salvador and Honduras started the infamous "Futbol War" after a violent World Cup qualifying match. The game followed months of tensions over migrant workers. More than 2,000 people were killed when El Salvador invaded Honduras.

A DIFFERENT GAME

Some people think that the solution to racism and xenophobia lies with the fans themselves. England fans have worked hard to improve the atmosphere at international matches, by laying out cards on all the seats in a stadium to create massive images of both sides' national flags; by inviting delegations of opposition fans over before the game to improve goodwill; and by trying to create a carnival atmosphere with the help of a supporters' brass band. More cynical commentators suggest that more effective policing and the threat of a ban from international competitions has led to a reduction in violence.

⬇ *Rioting England fans throw chairs in Charleroi, Belgium, during the 2000 European Championships. Events like this make it hard for England fans to lose their reputation as trouble-makers.*

WHEN ORGANISED *football first emerged in the 19th century no-one could have predicted how popular it would become. They would not have anticipated television and its effect on the sport, the huge success of the World Cup or the rise of millionaire players. At the start of the 21st century it is still hard to predict what will happen next in football, but some developments are more likely than others.*

HI-TECH FOOTBALL

Technology will continue to have an impact on football. Many people think that more stadiums will have retractable roofs to save games from bad weather. Another likely development is the introduction of smartcards – plastic cards with microchips. These cards could replace season tickets and provide clubs with more security – allowing them to know exactly when and where supporters enter the stadium.

➡ *Japanese fans support England at the World Cup 2002. Japan is one of the emerging new markets in football.*

NEW COUNTRIES

As the sport grows in popularity, more countries are likely to catch "football fever". Nations such as China, Japan, Australia and the USA present new markets for television companies wishing to broadcast matches and other companies wishing to use football to advertise their products. Some commentators predict that an Asian or African nation will win the World Cup in the 21st century. Such a win would only fuel the marketing opportunities and money associated with the sport.

⬅ *Modern stadiums with retractable roofs like this one will ensure that bad weather does not affect games.*

NEW CHALLENGES

There is a danger that the biggest clubs will continue to get richer, depriving other teams of money and attention. Some people suggest that football should adopt an idea from American basketball, in which the teams that finish bottom of the league have the pick of next season's transfers. This would mean that the best players do not automatically go to the clubs with the most money. Another risk is that TV coverage of football will reach saturation point, and broadcasters will turn to new sports. If this occurs, football must be able to survive without the money television brings.

FOOTBALL CRAZY

One thing that will not change is the drama of football. For football fans, nothing can beat the elation of watching a great goal being scored or the unexpected victory of a small side defeating one of the giant clubs. Players and teams might change, but the magic of "the beautiful game" will always remain.

GET THE FACTS STRAIGHT

- Football is now established as the world's number one sport.
- FIFA now has 204 member countries.
- FIFA's Goal Programme is helping financially disadvantaged associations in 165 nations.
- The Goal Programme includes building association headquarters, laying grass or artificial turf pitches, providing technical training centres and other basic amenities.
- One Goal initiative is helping to heal the scars of the recent civil conflict in the Solomon Islands in the South Pacific. It involves constructing goalposts from coconut shells and renovating the national stadium. The stadium is known as "The Garden of Eden". After the first game at the new stadium 3,000 fans lay down on the new pitch, stroked it and then started rolling on it!

GLOSSARY

administration: When a football club can not pay its debts it can declare itself bankrupt and be taken into administration. This means that many of its debts will never be fully paid, but a percentage of them will be offered to creditors.

agent: An agent acts on behalf of a footballer negotiating contracts and transfer deals. He or she often also handles players' media coverage and advertising deals. The agent receives a percentage of the player's earnings.

away kit: When teams play away from home they will change their kit if their usual colours clash with their opponent's kit. This is known as a second strip or away kit.

cup: A tournament where teams play each other on a knock-out basis. The winners of each game go through to the next round.

cup final: The final game between the last two sides left in a cup tournament.

gate: Used to describe the number of people who attend a game. A large gate is simply a large crowd.

group stage: A stage in some tournaments, such as the World Cup and European Champions League, where teams play each other in a mini-league before qualifying for the later knock-out stages.

hooligan: Term used to describe football supporters who fight or misbehave.

image rights: Players now sell the right to use their picture or autograph on everything, from clothes to computer games.

league: Where a group of clubs play each other over the course of a season. Points are awarded to indicate which team is the most successful and teams are positioned in a league table accordingly.

merchandising: Goods, from pens to clothes, created to sell because they are clearly linked with something popular, such as a football team or film.

promotion: When a team finishes in the top positions in the lower leagues they gain promotion to a higher league.

Public Limited Company (PLC): Clubs that become PLCs have shares that are quoted on the stock market. In theory, anyone with enough money can buy a share in them.

racism: Abuse of someone because of their nationality or skin colour.

red card: Card shown by referees when sending a player off the field for serious misconduct.

relegation: When teams finish in the bottom positions of a league they are relegated or demoted to the league below.

season: In football, each season generally lasts around nine months, say from August to May, and occurs over two calendar years. Thus we might refer to the 2003-04 season.

share price: The value of shares in a club that is a PLC, as traded on the stock markets.

signing-on fee: A sum given to football players when they join a new club.

sponsor: A business or organisation that pays a fee to have their name or brand linked with a club, often through shirt sponsorship.

super league: Informal term to describe the possible creation of a team featuring the best sides from European football.

television rights: Where broadcasting companies pay for the right to broadcast live games and/or highlights packages on television.

terraces: The standing areas at grounds. For safety reasons, many of these have been replaced by all-seater stands.

transfer: When a player moves between two clubs, usually for a fee.

yellow card: Card shown by referees for a bookable offence. If a player receives two yellow cards in one match he or she is shown a red card and sent off.

xenophobia: A fear or hatred of anything foreign.

FURTHER INFORMATION

The websites listed here will help you look further into football and the issues surrounding it. Many of these sites have links to other sites.

UK
British Council
The website run by the British Council looks at football culture around the world and also explores football trivia and some of the quirkier stories around football.
www.footballculture.net

The Football Association (FA)
The FA's official site contains issues from grass-roots clubs to the very top teams, plus news of women's football, the England international side and the FA Cup.
www.thefa.com

Similiar information can be found for Scotland, Wales and Northern Ireland at their associations' sites.

The Scottish Football Association (SFA)
www.scottishfa.co.uk

The Football Association of Wales (FAW)
www.faw.org.uk

The Irish Football Association
www.irishfa.com

FA Premier League
The FA Premiership's website has news of and links to all 20 English Premiership clubs.
www.premierleague.com

The Scottish Premier League
Information on the top league in Scotland with links to all 12 Premier League clubs.
www.scotprem.com

The Football League
The Football League's site has news from all 72 Football League clubs and history and statistics from the League.
www.football-league.co.uk

The Scottish Football League
Find out about the 30 clubs in the Scottish Football League at this site.
www.scottishfootballleague.com

AROUND THE WORLD
Australian Soccer Association (ASA)
News of the national side, the National Soccer League, women's football and Australian players abroad.
www.australiansoccer.com.au

Fédération Internationale de Football Association (FIFA)
News of past and future World Cups and of all FIFA's work. Details of the 204 national associations of FIFA.
www.fifa.com

Union of European Football Nations (UEFA)
UEFA's website has news of all UEFA competitions such as the European Champions League and UEFA Cup, video clips and news and statistics from every UEFA affiliated country.
www.uefa.com

World Soccer
The on-line edition of *World Soccer* magazine has news, interviews, opinions and statistics from all over the football world.
www.worldsoccer.com

FURTHER READING
If you are into football statistics and figures, you might want to look out for this book.

The Sky Sports Football Yearbook
(Headline)
This annual book has comprehensive statistics of every season, plus numerous records and statistics from domestic, European and international football

INDEX